YOUR
OTHER LEFT!

Punch Lines from the Front Lines

MICHAEL HIRSH

YOUR OTHER LEFT!

Punch Lines from the Front Lines

NEW AMERICAN LIBRARY

NEW AMERICAN LIBRARY
Published by New American Library, a division of
Penguin Group (USA) Inc., 375 Hudson Street, New York, New York 10014, U.S.A.
Penguin Books Ltd, 80 Strand, London WC2R 0RL, England
Penguin Books Australia Ltd, 250 Camberwell Road, Camberwell, Victoria 3124, Australia
Penguin Books Canada Ltd, 10 Alcorn Avenue, Toronto, Ontario, Canada M4V 3B2
Penguin Books (N.Z.) Ltd, Cnr Rosedale and Airborne Roads, Albany, Auckland 1310, New Zealand

Penguin Books Ltd, Registered Offices: 80 Strand, London WC2R 0RL, England

First published by New American Library, a division of Penguin Group (USA) Inc.

First Printing, May 2004
1 3 5 7 9 10 8 6 4 2

Copyright © Michael Hirsh, 2004
All rights reserved

 REGISTERED TRADEMARK—MARCA REGISTRADA

LIBRARY OF CONGRESS CATALOGING-IN-PUBLICATION DATA:

Hirsh, Michael, 1957–
Your other left! : punch lines from the front lines / Michael Hirsh.
p. cm.
ISBN 0-451-21212-6
1. United States—Armed Forces—Humor. 2. United States—Armed Forces—Military life. I. Title.
U766.H57 2004
355'.00973—dc22   2003025668

Printed in the United States of America

Dedicated to my buddies in the 25th Infantry Division PIO
Cu Chi, Vietnam (1966–67)

And to the American Red Cross Donut Dollies
who served with us and brightened every day—
especially to our favorite, Kaki (Kate) Lundy,
who still knows how to make us smile

*We were all kids who learned too young that if inappropriate
laughter can help make the pain go away,
it isn't inappropriate.*

I'll go out on a limb here and say that there is no other institution that generates more one-liners, more jokes, and more humor than the military. It begins with the stinging ridicule of the DI in boot camp, continues through battlefield jokes that dull the pain, and goes all the way to comments about what's likely to happen after retirement—if you live that long. A military career is inevitably punctuated and occasionally punctured with humor.

Part of what makes this possible is that good taste in humor is rarely an issue among military men and women. Living conditions and the food are often such that joking is the best way to survive them. Humor—sometimes black humor—is often the *only* way to endure the inherently dangerous nature of the job. And the occasional pomposity of the institution itself begs for someone to deflate it. Okay. So it's more than occasional.

Collected in *Your Other Left!: Punch Lines from the Front Lines,* are some of the best one-liners, training truisms, and parodies you've ever heard—or repeated. Many were found floating around the Internet; others were sent to me by military members who got wind of this project and wanted to pass theirs along, too. Feel free to tell any of these yourself, preferably at an inappropriate time. And if you've got a couple of jokes that belong in the next volume, don't hesitate to e-mail them to me. Never mind what the drill sergeant told you about being there to "defend democracy, not practice it." A little free speech is a good thing—especially if you can do it anonymously.

Michael Hirsh
Punta Gorda, Florida
April 1, 2004
UniformlyFunny@hirshmedia.us

ARMY

---

*NOTHING'S IMPOSSIBLE FOR
THOSE WHO DON'T HAVE TO DO IT.*

There is always a way, and it usually doesn't work.

Bravery is being the only one who knows you're afraid.

There is no such thing as a perfect plan.

Friendly fire—isn't.

Suppressive fire—won't.

If the enemy is in range, so are you.

It's not the one with your name on it, it's the one addressed "to whom it may concern" you've got to think about.

Whenever you have plenty of ammo, you never miss. Whenever you are low on ammo, you can't hit the broad side of a barn.

TRY TO LOOK UNIMPORTANT; THE ENEMY MAY BE LOW ON AMMO.

"Sometimes I think war is God's way of teaching us geography."
—Paul Rodriguez

"Nothing in life is so exhilarating as to be shot at without result."
—Winston Churchill

"Whoever said 'the pen is mightier than the sword' obviously
never encountered automatic weapons."
—Gen. Douglas MacArthur

Anything You Do Can Get You Killed, Including Nothing.

The enemy invariably attacks on two occasions:

1

When they're ready.

2

When you're not.

No plan ever survives initial contact with the enemy.

Make it too tough for the enemy to get in, and you won't
be able to get out.

EVERY COMMAND THAT CAN BE MISUNDERSTOOD WILL BE.

THE SELF-IMPORTANCE OF A SUPERIOR IS INVERSELY PROPORTIONAL TO HIS POSITION IN THE HIERARCHY.

Radios will fail as soon as you need fire support.

Radar tends to fail at night and in bad weather, and especially during both.

Interchangeable parts—aren't.

The complexity of a weapon is inversely proportional to the IQ of the weapon's operator.

When reviewing the radio frequencies you just wrote down, the most important ones are always illegible.

If it's stupid but it works, it isn't stupid.

Never forget that your weapon was made by the lowest bidder.

Things that must be shipped together as a set aren't.

Things that must work together can't be carried to the field that way.

IF YOU TAKE MORE THAN YOUR FAIR SHARE OF OBJECTIVES, YOU WILL GET MORE THAN YOUR FAIR SHARE OF OBJECTIVES TO TAKE.

14

There are three kinds of men. The ones who learn by reading. The few who learn by observation. The rest of them have to pee on the electric fence.

A Purple Heart just proves that you were smart enough to think of a plan, stupid enough to try it, and lucky enough to survive.

Anything worth fighting for is worth fighting dirty for.

The Pentagon once did a study on why so many American servicemen marry women in the countries where they're stationed. Contrary to popular belief, loneliness has nothing to do with it. Once the men rotated back to the U.S., all their in-laws were thousands of miles away.

The enemy never watches until you make a mistake.

You can always tell a man who's been in the service. He can't understand the fascination people have with wearing camouflage clothing, driving Hummers, or playing with guns.

If you think sex is exciting, try incoming.

IF AT FIRST YOU DON'T SUCCEED, THEN BOMB DISPOSAL PROBABLY ISN'T FOR YOU.

IF YOUR ATTACK IS GOING REALLY WELL, IT'S AN AMBUSH.

Never share a foxhole with anyone braver than yourself.

The enemy diversion you are ignoring is their main attack.

If you are forward of your position, your artillery will fall short.

To be sure of hitting the target, shoot first, then call whatever you hit "The Target."

Once the pin is pulled, Mr. Grenade is no longer your friend.

Five-second fuses always burn three seconds.

The bursting radius of a hand grenade is always one foot greater than your jumping range.

The Ranger captain was explaining to his company a new program to use DoD schools to help eradicate illiteracy, improve linguistics, and enhance communication and interpersonal skills among the men. "What do you think about that?" he asked. "Hoooah!" they shouted.

Don't look conspicuous; it draws fire, which irritates everyone around you.

When you have secured the area, make sure the enemy knows it, too.

Incoming fire has the right of way.

The only thing more accurate than incoming enemy fire is incoming friendly fire.

The best armor is staying out of gunshot range.

Tracer bullets work in both directions.

BEER MATH

2 beers x 37 men = 49 cases

BODY COUNT MATH

3 guerrillas + 1 probable + 2 pigs = 37 enemy KIA

A clean and dry set of BDUs is a magnet for mud and rain.

As soon as you are served hot chow in the field, it rains.

One of the worst jobs in the military is being a cook. They have enemies on both sides of any war.

THE JOURNEY OF A THOUSAND MILES BEGINS WITH ONE STEP—AND A LOT OF BITCHING.

The easy way is always mined.

If you can't remember, the claymore is pointed toward you.

Whenever you drop your equipment in a firefight, your ammo and grenades always fall the farthest away, and your canteen always lands at your feet.

Guard: "Halt! Who goes there?"

FNG: "Aw, you wouldn't know me. I just got here today."

If you need an officer in a hurry, take a nap.

Never trust a private with a loaded weapon or an officer with a map.

A personnel clerk at Fort Meade received a document, initialed it, and passed it on to the duty officer. It promptly came back with a note attached: "This document didn't concern you. Erase your initials and initial the erasure."

You have exceeded the maximum effective range of an excuse.

A military woman wrote: "We have women in the infantry, but they don't intentionally put us on the front lines. Why? They don't know if we can fight, if we can kill. I think we can. All the general has to do is walk over to the women and say, 'You see the enemy over there? They say you look fat in those uniforms.' "

The problem with the Iraqi army is that they use
Russian defense tactics:

1
Engage the enemy.

2
Draw him into your territory.

3
Wait until winter sets in.

We are not retreating; we are advancing in another direction.

The most dangerous thing in the world is a second lieutenant
with a map and a compass.

A motor pool sergeant commenting on a newly assigned private: "If I could buy that guy for what he's worth and sell him for what he thinks he's worth, I could retire."

Success occurs when no one is looking; failure occurs when the general is watching.

To all ladies: Marry an Army veteran. He can cook. He can make a bed. He can sew. And he is already used to taking orders.

If you think it's really true that, as General MacArthur said, old soldiers fade away, ask any of them to put on their old Army uniforms.

A retired sergeant was asked, "Well, how do you like civilian life?" "Terrible," he replied gruffly. "All those people around and nobody in charge."

BRITISH MILITARY PERFORMANCE REPORTS

His men would follow him anywhere, but only out of curiosity.

This officer is really not so much of a has-been, but more of a definitely won't-be.

When she opens her mouth, it seems that this is only to change whichever foot was previously in there.

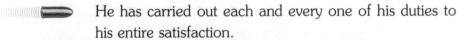 He has carried out each and every one of his duties to his entire satisfaction.

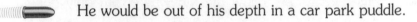 He would be out of his depth in a car park puddle.

This young lady has delusions of adequacy.

Since my last report he has reached rock bottom—and has started to dig.

She sets low personal standards and then consistently fails to achieve them.

He has the wisdom of youth and the energy of old age.

In my opinion, this pilot should not be authorized to fly below 250 feet.

This man is depriving a village somewhere of its idiot.

Works well when under constant supervision and cornered like a rat in a trap.

IF AT FIRST YOU
DON'T SUCCEED,
CALL IN AN AIR STRIKE.

NATO excuse for bombing the wrong target: Headquarters' dinner order for "take-out Chinese" was grossly misunderstood.

The FNG about to take his first helicopter ride asked the crew chief why the choppers didn't have doors. Crew chief: "If they wanted them to be safe, they'd be called Volvos."

If the wings are traveling faster than the fuselage, it's probably a helicopter—and therefore unsafe.

If you push the cyclic forward, the houses get bigger. If you pull the cyclic back, they get smaller. (Unless you keep pulling it back—then they get bigger again.)

The rotor system is just a big fan on top of the helicopter to keep the pilot cool. Want proof? Make it stop; then watch the pilot break out into a sweat.

Takeoffs are optional. Landings are mandatory.

Flying is the second greatest thrill known to man.
Landing is the first.

Everyone already knows the definition of a *good* landing is one from which you can walk away. But very few know the definition of a *great* landing. It's one after which you can use the helicopter another time.

It's best to keep the pointed end going forward as much as possible.

Never let a helicopter take you somewhere your brain didn't get to five minutes earlier.

HELICOPTERS CAN'T REALLY FLY—THEY'RE JUST SO UGLY THAT THE EARTH IMMEDIATELY REPELS THEM.

Speed is life. Altitude is life insurance. No one has ever collided with the sky.

The only time you have too much fuel is when you're on fire.

No matter which way you have to march, it's always uphill.

If God had meant for us to be in the Army, we would have
been born with green, baggy skin.

Q: How is being in the army like an orgasm?
A: The closer you get to discharge, the better you feel.

NAVY &
COAST GUARD

ANY SHIP CAN BE A MINESWEEPER—
ONCE.

NAVY PILOTS PRAYER:

God grant me the eyes of an eagle,
The stealth of a stalking tiger,
And the balls of an Army helicopter pilot.

When a young sailor is having problems, they can generally be attributed to money and liberty. The two must be kept in balance. Too much of one and not enough of the other will always spell trouble.

THERE ARE MORE PLANES
IN THE OCEAN
THAN THERE ARE
SHIPS IN THE SKY.

Officer: Sailor, do you have change for a dollar?
Sailor: Sure, buddy.
Officer: That's no way to address an officer. Now let's try
again. Sailor, do you have change for a dollar?
Sailor: No, sir!

Keep looking around; there's always something you missed.

A woman married to a Navy pilot inquired about an increase in their monthly allotment for living quarters, as rents near the station where he was based were so high. She received the following letter back: "Class Q allotments are based upon the number of dependents, up to a maximum of three. If the birth of a child will mean your husband is entitled to more quarters allowance, please notify him to take the necessary action required."

There are basically two types of ships at sea: submarines and targets.

Things you don't want to hear in a submarine: "Captain, the flooding put out the fire."

FROM THE U.S. COAST GUARD:

- We take more breaks by 0800 than most people will take all day.

- If it's not broke, mess with it until it is.

- Lesson #1 for ship drivers: If your draft is greater than your freeboard, you are sinking.

MARINES

*ALWAYS REMEMBER TO
PILLAGE BEFORE YOU BURN.*

The reason why the Army, Navy, Marines, and Air Force bicker among themselves is that they don't speak the same language. For instance, take the simple phrase "secure the building."

The Army will post guards around the place.

The Navy will turn out the lights and lock the doors.

The Marines will kill everybody inside and set up a headquarters.

The Air Force will take out a five-year lease with an option to buy.

No combat-ready unit has ever passed inspection.

Teamwork is essential; it gives the enemy other people to shoot at.

THE FIVE MOST DANGEROUS THINGS IN THE MARINE CORPS:

A private saying, "I just got the word."

A sergeant saying, "Lock and load."

A second lieutenant saying, "Follow me."

A captain saying to an inbound A-6, "Our position is . . ."

A lieutenant colonel saying, "I've seen this shit before. . . ."

If you find yourself in a hole, stop digging.

Never miss a good chance to shut up.

One Marine recruit found that all of the uniforms he was issued fit him perfectly. So he began to worry that he was deformed.

The quartermaster has only two sizes—too large and too small.

UNOFFICIAL MARINE CORPS EXPLANATION OF THE GENEVA CONVENTION TO RECRUITS: "THEY CAN KILL YOU BUT THEY CAN'T EAT YOU."

A lieutenant asked a Marine why he was falling back during a really fierce battle. "Did you hear me say that we're outnumbered four to one?"

The Marine replied, "I got my four, sir!"

Basic-training recruit: "I can't bounce a quarter off this bed, sir."

"Why not?"

"If you've got change for a dollar, I can show you."

"All right, you bastards, fall in—on the double!" barked the sergeant as he strode into the barracks. Each Marine grabbed his hat and jumped to his feet, except one—a private who lay in his bunk reading a book. "Well?" roared the sergeant. "Well," observed the private, "there certainly are a lot of them, aren't there?"

AIR FORCE

CLUSTER BOMBING FROM B-52S
IS VERY, VERY ACCURATE.
THE BOMBS ARE GUARANTEED TO
ALWAYS HIT THE GROUND.

It is generally inadvisable to eject over the territory you just bombed.

Our bombs are smarter than the average high school student.
At least they know how to find Baghdad.

WHO CARES IF A LASER-GUIDED 500-POUND BOMB IS ACCURATE TO WITHIN NINE FEET?

A fighter pilot is a confused soul who talks about women when he's flying, and about flying when he's womanizing.

Q: How do you know if a fighter pilot's in a bar?
A: He'll tell you.

HOW TO BE ANNOYING DURING THE AIR FORCE MANDATORY STATIONARY BIKE TEST:

1

Wear a bike helmet to the test. Optional: include knee and elbow pads.

2

Demand the tester wear a reflective road guard vest or belt "for safety."

3

Bring a bike horn and attach it. Each time the tester adjusts the tension, honk the horn loudly and yell, "Get the hell out of the way, you idiot."

4

Attach streamers to the handgrips.

5

Bring a playing card to the test. Demand that it be inserted in the spokes.

6

Pop a wheelie.

7
Signal all turns.

8
Make motorcycle sounds. Be sure to shift gears when the tester changes the tension.

9
Bring a sack of newspapers. Deliver them.

10

Periodically extend your arms and legs, yelling,
"Look, Ma, no hands!"

11

Bring a friend to ride on the handlebars.

12

Attach a kiddie seat to the back. Bring your kid.

13

Bring a bike lock. Be sure to secure the bike when you leave.

ANY ATTEMPT TO STRETCH FUEL IS GUARANTEED TO INCREASE HEADWIND.

Conversation overheard on an Air Force base between two pilots about to retire: "Being an airline pilot would be great if you didn't have to go on all those trips."

What's the similarity between air traffic controllers and pilots? If a pilot screws up, the pilot dies. If ATC screws up, the pilot dies.

Truly superior pilots use their superior judgment to avoid those situations where they might have to use their superior skills.

Learn from the mistakes of others. You won't live long enough to make all of them yourself.

AIR FORCE VARIATIONS ON WHY THE CHICKEN CROSSED THE ROAD:

Colonel: Successful crossing, well planned, and carried out in accordance with my directives.

Chief: About time that thing worked; hope the colonel's finally happy.

NCO: Changed two wings and a beak, and removed a bad egg. Damn thing still won't fly.

2nd Lt.: Look at the pretty bird!

Tower: The chicken was instructed to hold short of the road. This road-incursion incident was reported in a Hazardous Chicken Road-Crossing Report (HCRCR). Please reemphasize that chickens are required to read back all "hold short" instructions.

Command Post: What chicken?

Air Education and Training Command (AETC): The purpose is to familiarize the chicken with road-crossing procedures. Road crossing should be performed only between the hours of sunset and sunrise. Solo chickens must have at least three miles of visibility and a safety observer.

Air Force Special Operations Command (AFSOC): The chicken crossed at a 90-degree angle to avoid prolonged exposure to a line of communication. To achieve maximum surprise, the chicken should perform this maneuver at night using NVGs, preferably near a road bend in a valley.

Air Force Personnel Center (AFPC): Due to the needs of the Air Force, the chicken was involuntarily reassigned to the other side of the road. This will be a three-year controlled tour, and we promise to give the chicken a good-deal assignment afterward. Every chicken will be required to do one road crossing during its career, and this will not affect its opportunities for promotion.

Defense Intelligence Agency (DIA): Despite what you see on CNN, I can neither confirm nor deny any fowl performing acts of transit.

C-130 Crew Member: Just put the damn bird in the back and let's go.

C-141 Crew Member: I ordered a #4 with turkey and ham, *not* chicken! Besides, where the heck are my condiments? We ain't taking off till I get my @%#*#@! condiments!

AWACS Crew: Due to our being in a turn at that precise moment, we have no confirmation of any chickens in the area at that time.

F-117 Stealth Pilot: Wasn't that great? I snuck up on it at two feet AGL at 480 knots, illuminated its tail feathers with the laser designator, and goosed it before it even knew I was there.

ALL-WEATHER CLOSE AIR SUPPORT DOESN'T WORK IN BAD WEATHER.

Gravity never loses. The best you can hope for is a draw.

Remember, gravity is not just a good idea. It's the law.

The fighter pilot's breakfast—two aspirin, a cup of coffee, and a puke.

What's the difference between God and fighter pilots?
God doesn't think he's a fighter pilot.

It's a good landing if you can still get the doors open.

You know you've landed with the wheels up when it takes full power to taxi.

GOOD JUDGMENT COMES FROM EXPERIENCE. EXPERIENCE COMES FROM BAD JUDGMENT.

USAF MAINTENANCE LOGS:

Problem: Left inside main tire almost needs replacement.
Solution: Almost replaced left inside main tire.

Problem: Test flight OK, except autoland very rough.
Solution: Autoland not installed on this aircraft.

Problem #1: Number 2 propeller seeping prop fluid.
Solution #1: Number 2 propeller seepage normal.
Problem #2: Numbers 1, 3, and 4 propellers lack normal seepage.

Problem: Something loose in cockpit.
Solution: Something tightened in cockpit.

Problem: Evidence of hydraulic leak on right main landing gear.
Solution: Evidence removed.

Problem: DME volume unbelievably loud.
Solution: Volume set to more believable level.

Problem: Autopilot in altitude hold mode produced a 200 fpm descent.
Solution: Cannot reproduce problem on ground.

Problem: Target radar hums.
Solution: Reprogrammed target radar with lyrics.

Problem: Dead bugs on windshield.
Solution: Live bugs on backorder.

Problem: IFF (Identify Friend or Foe beacon) inoperative.
Solution: IFF inoperative in OFF mode.

Problem: Aircraft handles funny.
Solution: Aircraft warned to straighten up, fly right, and be serious.

Problem: Friction locks cause throttle levers to stick.
Solution: That is what they are there for.

Problem: Number three engine missing.
Solution: Engine found on right wing after brief search.

A thunderstorm is never as bad on the inside as it appears on the outside. It's worse.

It's always better to be down here wishing you were up there, than up there wishing you were down here.

**DON'T DROP THE AIRCRAFT
IN ORDER TO FLY THE
MICROPHONE.
AN AIRPLANE FLIES
BECAUSE OF A PRINCIPLE
DISCOVERED BY BERNOULLI,
NOT MARCONI.**

The most famous last words in military aviation:

1

"Why is it doing that?"

2

"Where are we?"

3

"Oh, shiiiiit!"

IFR: I follow roads.

Stay out of the clouds. The silver lining everyone keeps talking about might be another airplane going in the opposite direction. Reliable sources also report that mountains have been known to hide out in clouds.

THINGS WHICH DO YOU NO GOOD IN AVIATION:

Altitude above you.

Runway behind you.

Fuel in the truck.

At 90-degrees angle of bank, the lift slides off the wings.

The probability of survival is equal to the angle of arrival.

Long ago, a C-124 and an F-4 fighter were on intersecting
taxiways at Rhein-Main airfield. The F-4 driver asked Ground
what the Globemaster's intentions were. It is said that the C-124
pilot opened the clamshell doors in the nose and announced,
"I'm going to eat you."

AIR FORCE DICTIONARY

BLAMESTORMING—Sitting around the squadron discussing why a mission failed and who was responsible.

SEAGULL COLONEL—A colonel who swoops in, makes a lot of noise, and dumps stuff all over everything.

SALMON DAY—The experience of spending the entire day swimming upstream only to get screwed and die in the end.

$\sqrt{106}$

ASSMOSIS—The process by which some people seem to absorb success and promotability by kissing up to the commander.

CRM (CAREER RESTRICTING MOVE)—Used among officers to describe ill-advised activity, as in "Trashing core values while your commander is within earshot is serious CRM."

ADMINISPHERE—The rarified organizational layers beginning just above wing level. Decisions that fall from the adminisphere are generally profoundly inappropriate or irrelevant to the problems they were designed to solve.

DILBERTED—To be exploited and oppressed by your boss. Derived from the experiences of Dilbert, the geek-in-hell comic strip character. "I've been dilberted again. The old man changed my leave schedule for the fourth time this month."

FLIGHT RISK—Used to describe troops who are suspected of planning to retire or separate from the service soon. Alternatively, any O-6 or above who gets behind the controls of an airplane.

GENERICA—Features of the Air Force landscape that are exactly the same no matter which base one is at, such as Burger King, Robin Hood, and the BX and AMX terminal. Used as in, "We were so lost in generica that I forgot what base we were at."

PERCUSSIVE MAINTENANCE—The fine art of whacking the crap out of a $200,000 inertial navigation unit to get it to work again.

Faith is believing in something common sense tells us not to.

If enough data is collected, a board of inquiry can prove anything.

War does not determine who is right; war determines who is left.

Professional soldiers are predictable; it's the amateurs who are dangerous.

And finally, for those reading this book who have yet to experience the joys of deployment we offer this
GUIDE TO PREPARING FOR DEPLOYMENT TO OPERATION IRAQI FREEDOM/OPERATION ENDURING FREEDOM

The following are things you can do once you get your deployment notice to make your transition from home easier:

1
Sleep on a cot in the garage

2
Replace the garage door with a curtain

3

Six hours after you go to sleep, have your wife, husband, or significant other whip open the curtain, shine a flashlight in your eyes, and mumble, "Sorry, wrong cot."

4

Renovate your bathroom. Hang a green plastic sheet down the middle of your bathtub and move the showerhead down to chest level. Keep four inches of soapy cold water on the floor.

5

Put lube oil in your humidifier instead of water and set it to "High" for that tactical generator smell.

6

Don't watch TV except for movies in the middle of the night.
Have your family vote on which movie to watch—
then watch a different one.

7

Leave lawnmower running in your living room 24 hours a day for proper noise level.

8

Have the paperboy give you a haircut.

9

Make up and post your family menu a week ahead of time
without looking in your pantry or refrigerator. Then serve some
kind of meat in an unidentifiable sauce poured over noodles.
Do this for every meal.

10

Once a month take every major appliance completely apart and then put them back together.

11

Use 18 scoops of coffee per pot and allow it to sit for five or six hours before drinking.

12

Invite at least 185 people you don't really like because they have strange personal hygiene habits to come and visit for a couple of months. Exchange clothes with them.

13

Raise the thresholds and lower the top sills on your front and back doors so that you either trip over the threshold or hit your head on the sill every time you pass through one of them.

14

Keep a roll of toilet paper on your nightstand and bring it to the bathroom with you. Also bring a weapon and a flashlight.

15

Drink your milk and sodas warm.

16

Go to the bathroom when you just have gas, "just in case."
Every time.

17

Announce to your family they have mail, have them report to you as you stand outside your open garage door after supper, and then say, "Sorry, it's for the other Smith."

18

Wash only fifteen items of laundry this week. Roll up the semi-wet clean clothes in a ball and place them in a cloth sack in the corner of the garage where the cat pees. After a week, unroll them, and without ironing or removing the mildew, proudly wear them to professional meetings and family gatherings.
Pretend you don't know what you look or smell like.

19

Go to the worst crime-infested place near you. Go heavily armed, wearing a flak jacket and Kevlar helmet. Set up shop in a tent in a vacant lot. Announce to the local residents that you are there to help them.

20

Demand each family member be limited to ten minutes per week on the phone for a morale call. Enforce this with your teenage daughter.

21

Shoot a few bullet holes in the walls of your home
for proper ambiance.

22

Sandbag the floor of your car to protect youself from mine
blasts and fragmentation.

23

Fire off fifty cherry bombs simultaneously in your driveway at 0300. When startled neighbors appear, tell them it's all okay—you're just registering mortars. Tell them plastic will make an acceptable substitute for their broken windows.

24

Make your family dig a survivability position with overhead cover in the backyard. Complain that the 4x4s are not 8 inches on center and make them rebuild it.

Michael Hirsh is a Vietnam combat veteran (25th Inf. Div. PIO, Cu Chi, '66), a journalist, and a George Foster Peabody Award–winning documentary filmmaker. He is currently collecting military jokes for a sequel to *Your Other Left*. E-mail submissions to UniformlyFunny@ hirshmedia.us.